Animal Groups

Amphibians

By Dalton Rains

www.littlebluehousebooks.com

Copyright © 2024 by Little Blue House, Mendota Heights, MN 55120. All rights reserved. No part of this book may be reproduced or utilized in any form or by any means without written permission from the publisher.

Little Blue House is distributed by North Star Editions:
sales@northstareditions.com | 888-417-0195

Produced for Little Blue House by Red Line Editorial.

Photographs ©: Shutterstock Images, cover, 4 (top), 4 (bottom), 7 (top), 7 (bottom), 8–9, 11, 13, 15, 17, 19, 21, 22 (water background), 22 (salamander life cycle), 23, 24 (top left), 24 (top right), 24 (bottom left), 24 (bottom right)

Library of Congress Control Number: 2022919942

ISBN
978-1-64619-806-1 (hardcover)
978-1-64619-835-1 (paperback)
978-1-64619-892-4 (ebook pdf)
978-1-64619-864-1 (hosted ebook)

Printed in the United States of America
Mankato, MN
082023

About the Author

Dalton Rains writes and edits nonfiction children's books. He lives in Minnesota.

Table of Contents

Water and Land **5**

Is It an Amphibian? **22**

Glossary **24**

Index **24**

Water and Land

Some animals are amphibians. They live in water and on land.

Toads are amphibians.

The toad has bumps.

Frogs are amphibians too.

Their skin is smooth.

7

Salamanders are amphibians. They have long tails and smooth skin.

Newts are amphibians.

The newt has orange skin.

Amphibians start as eggs. The frog lays eggs in water.

Then the eggs hatch.
Baby frogs are
called tadpoles.
Tadpoles have tails.

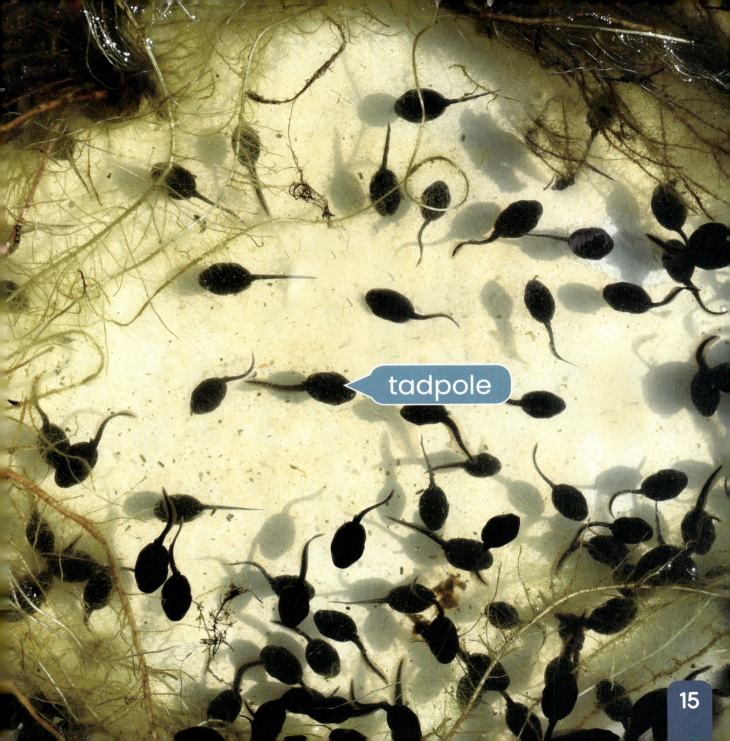

Tadpoles live in the water.

Soon they grow legs.

Tadpoles grow into adults. Adult frogs can leave the water.

Adult amphibians can be in water or on land.
The salamander swims.

Is It an Amphibian?

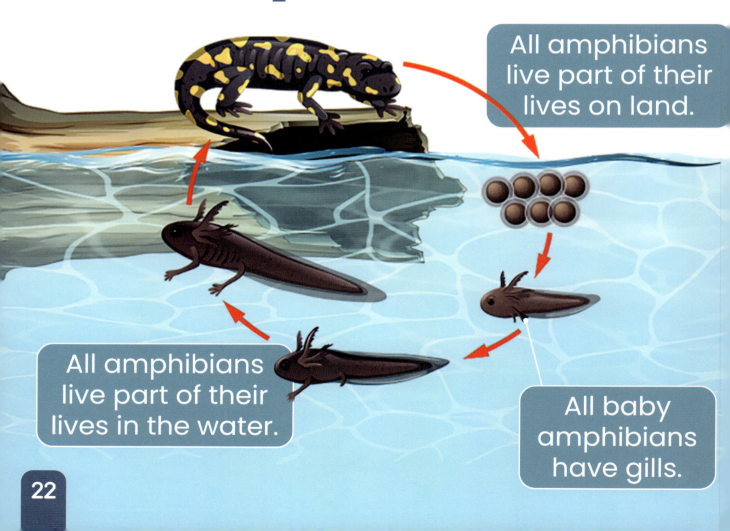

All amphibians live part of their lives on land.

All amphibians live part of their lives in the water.

All baby amphibians have gills.

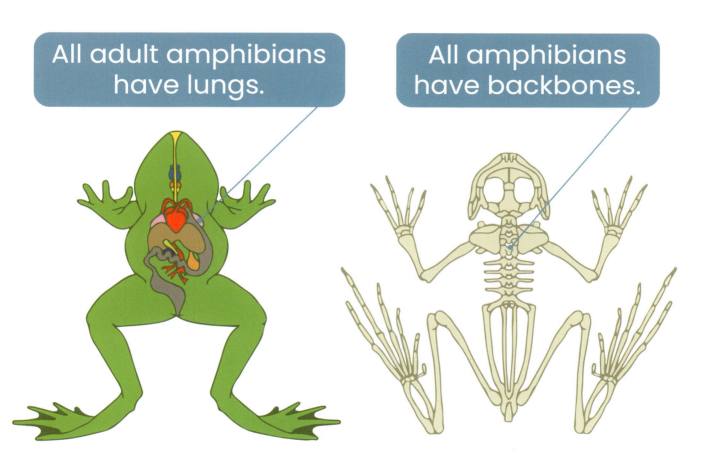

Glossary

newt

tadpoles

salamander

toad

Index

E
eggs, 12, 14

H
hatch, 14

L
legs, 16

T
tails, 8, 14